THE SECRET

THE SECRET

ARTHUR DAVISON FICKE

THE SECRET
And Other Poems

Garden City, New York

Doubleday, Doran & Company, Inc.

1936

PRINTED AT THE *Country Life Press*, GARDEN CITY, N. Y., U. S. A.

ACKNOWLEDGMENT *is made to the editors of the following magazines for courteous permission to reprint a number of the included poems: Scribner's Magazine, The Saturday Review of Literature, The New Yorker, The Westminster Magazine, The Forum, Poetry, Contemporary Vision, The Children's Bookshelf, Harper's Magazine, The American Mercury, Esquire, The Poet and Critic, The American Girl, The Musical Courier, The Woman's Home Companion, The Delineator, Voices.*

CONTENTS

vii

viii

I: THE SECRET

THE SECRET

MY FRIEND, will you take me by the hand
And refrain from making easy fun of me
If I speak to you frankly and ramblingly of the confusions,
(Mine and yours, both,)
The moral doubts, the personal fears, the chaos of purposes
Which, for me at least, make the raucous music
That our day plays for us
While we, with what dignity we can,
Dance our ceremonious dance called the Dance of Death?

Today as I sit, quiet and brooding,
Here on a high hill overlooking miles of Maytime valley,
And the beauty of the flowers is beginning again,
And the loathsome tent-worms are, as in no year past,
Destroying all that is fair, stripping the trees to winter
    nakedness—
Here I wonder whether my nightmares are merely the
    dreams of a weakling
And whether stronger and nobler men than I see a different
    vision.

If I am to speak to you at all, my friend,
It must be frankly.
So I tell you in advance that I have a lifelong Secret.
It is deeply buried—and all my days, all these fifty-two years,
I have tried to discover that Secret.
For I do not know what it is:
I merely know that it is there.
Nothing in the outside world can attract my attention for an
    instant
Unless it is in some way revelatory and symbolic of that
    Secret.
Wars, revolutions, politics,
Vast economic changes, tremendous scientific discoveries,
Earthquakes and famines and royal marriages,
These may come and go, leaving me unmoved and unin-
    terested
Unless they whisper to me something about my Secret.

My Secret concerns some profound enigma:
It has to do with the nature of the heart of man
And the conditions of his essential happiness.
It is a thing wholly within, wholly private and of the lonely
    spirit;
The changes of mere events are not of its world.
Sometimes I almost find a clue to it
In a book or a painting or the words of a friend;

4

But still it eludes me.
If I knew it, I would tell it to you with joy,
In the hope that it would be your Secret, also,
And that you would be happy to have your Secret made
    clear to you
And to have it shared by another.
But I do not know my Secret,
And it may be that I shall never discover it.

(3)

I wonder whether we of today are alone in our confusions?
I wonder whether all people, always,
Have not been ill at ease in the centuries into which they
    were born?
Did not Walter Scott hunger for the Feudal Ages,
And did not William Blake lust for a Paradise
Where there was one Serpent and one Naked Woman,
And did not Goethe believe that the ancient Greeks were a
    pleasant people?
Are the confusions really worse today,
Or is it merely that it is we who now suffer from them?
The Thirty Years War could not have been a nice epoch,
    for quiet persons;
And there was a period, while Rome tottered,
That could hardly have been reassuring to anyone but the
    Goths.

I suspect that I am not alone in my loneliness,
And that many minds are asking the same question that I ask,
And that many eyes stare into the same vacancy that I
    see.
The world is loud with the voices
Of persons who assert that they know everything;
But there are also silent places
Where unspoken questions hang quivering in the air.

I cannot disclose to you your Secret nor my own.
But this I can say with certainty.—
I beg you, my friend, to build up no wall
Between yourself and other men
Or between yourself and your Secret.
To do so would be easier, perhaps happier,
But it would not be wise.
Neither from within nor from without can we accept final
    defeat.
No, in spite of confusions—
No, though all the confusions hurl themselves upon us in
    our weakest moment
They shall not prevail.
You have your Secret: follow it, discover it,
Hold it sacred through all the clamors and all the silences.

6

For the voices of terror are with us,
And who is so strong that he can hold himself unshaken by
    fear and pity
When they speak?

   I recall a rainy night, late, in New York.
As I rode through the shiny black streets in my taxi
I asked the driver questions, as I always do,
About life and death and himself.

   He had a dark, sensitive face.
He said: "Me, mister?   Yes, I'm an American.
I was born on the East Side, and I haven't ever been
More than twenty miles away from Times Square.
You can see that I'm a Jew, can't you?   But just the same
    I'm an American.
And I tell you, mister, that there is no longer
Any beauty or honor left in my country,
And I wish that I were dead."

   I could not answer.
He left me at the door of my hotel
And whirled away into the chaos of the night.

   One evening in a charming dining-room
Where twelve people were talking, over their food and wine,

A lady said to me:
"I don't know how these working-people
Expect us to be able to give them employment
If they keep on asking such ridiculous wages
And if we have to pay such big income-taxes."
I did not reply, for I knew that the lady owned acres of mills
And hundreds of workingmen's houses; and my reflections
    were unpleasant.
But perhaps I did her an injustice—for today
She is penniless, and her two thousand mill-employes
Stalk desperate in the silence of that mill-town—
Except for a favored few, who are growing fat
In the sunlight transmitted from Washington to sterling
    party-members.

(8)

    And one of my friends was battered into a pulp by the
        police
Because he dared to say in Indiana
That it is indecent to starve men and women and children
Who work in factories.
And the nations are arming for more carnage.
And the rich men are scurrying about, predatory or fright-
    ened,
Like foxes or rabbits or wolves or monkeys.
And no man who is both good and wise has yet spoken.

8

I, like you, my friend, see much—and am powerless.
I see the desperate houses of coal-miners in Pennsylvania
And the bleak homesteads of farmers in Iowa.
I see the faces of hopeless men in the streets of New York
And the faces of lazy men everywhere who are fattening on
the nation, like tent-worms.
The politicians run about making noises like hollow gourds
that have gall-stones inside them,
And the wisdom of today is the manifest folly of tomorrow.
I hear of a great hope in Russia, and also of a great despair;
Echoes come to me of an ideal, and also of a bloodthirsty
tyranny.
And my Secret has not spoken to me of these things,
And I am without guidance, in a day of general darkness
and mist.

(9)

An old farmer whom I know
Was sitting quietly on his porch
As I approached his house
To ask if I could buy some milk from him.

I said: "Good evening, Mr Denkmann!
I suppose that you are taking a little rest
After your hard day's work?"
He looked up at me from filmed eyes
That had seen six decades of toil;
He replied: "I do not work; I do not rest; I just wait."

I felt that if he would speak, he could tell me more of my
  Secret
Than all the rest of them put together.
But I was aware that Mr Denkmann, like you and myself,
Did not know his Secret.

(10)

It is because of this that many of us must move with
  timorous footsteps.
Men who have no undiscovered Secret in their hearts
Can advance boldly into the world of action—
Cheerleaders who know not and care not what the cheering
  is for.
These are the great men,
Who deal with events as the blacksmith deals with iron.
They look outward, they see the glowing metal on the anvil,
They strike firmly and violently, and they note that the
  shape of the metal is changed.
The delight of the powerful arm-muscles, the sense of
  dominating the iron,
These things are enough for outward-looking men.
But for men who have an undiscovered Secret, they are not
  enough.
And such a man will sometimes look at the iron for a long
  time in silence
And then turn away, unable to touch the metal until the full
  nature of his Secret shall become known to him.

10

And that is why a Secret is so perilous a companion;
For until our Secret has spoken, we dare not speak.
We do not know what it may reveal when it utters itself;
And if we should have erred, in the meantime,
Then when it spoke
Our minds would be instantly blown into fragments
Never recoverable.

If you, my friend, also have a Secret that will not yet
　　speak to you,
Do not despair.
Perhaps in the loneliness of some terrible midnight,
Or in the freshness of some windy dawn upon the hills,
Or in a quiet room where a friend takes your hand in com-
　　passion,
Or perhaps in the crowded noise of a city street when you
　　stare bewildered
Into the faces of hundreds of hurrying strangers—
Perhaps in one of these places, sometime, somehow,
Your Secret will suddenly rise up before you with shining
　　eyes
And say: "Behold!　I am I!　Follow Me!"

II: HOSPITAL

HOSPITAL

AS the first whirl of the anaesthetic came
I fought it
being too proud to surrender even into these desired arms
again it came
and again I repulsed so paltry a conqueror
you must do better than that   I said
for I am I

I strangled a little
"breathe deep!"   said the bored unkind voice of the anaes-
     thetist
I puffed out my belly vastly to show the brute how deep I
     was breathing

then it came
the great power swept me in a wave
while out of calm worlds of sanity I still heard the unper-
     turbed voice
of my friend the famous surgeon   saying
"I shall require the arm-rest here on the right side   Miss
     Heath
Dr Morris   you will be at my left   Dr Jamieson oppo-
     site"

a daze swept by   but it could not fool me
for I knew that the perfect silence was still far away
and that certain hells lay between

two stars burning furiously and approaching with the speed
    of light
left me still incredulous
but when I heard the click-click-click   clickety-click
of the monotonous gears of eternity
then I began to believe

                        and the well-known precise voice
out of long ago   saying as over a telephone "Number-two-
    four-two-eight please"
gave me hope that the end was near   and then
the voice of Eugen Boissevain as if directly inside my ear said
"you see now that there are many modes of being
and that all you have to do is choose which level you prefer
and stay there"
I realized that this was true
I was deeply interested in this tremendous thought
my God   it's indeed perfectly possible to cease to be human
and become a color or a stone or a point in space
or a proposition of Euclid   or what you will

suddenly force seized me and whirled me twice or thrice in
    the void
while I vainly struggled to regain equilibrium

then my soul said   oh merciful oblivion   merciful extinc-
      tion
it is you   it is you   it is you
and with a cold deadly effort of will
I resigned my will   I became the darkness

in that darkness someone lifted up my right arm to its full
      length
I resented the intrusion

then I entered suddenly into the paradise of non-being
then I inherited the ancient silence

(2)

no   it's all right   nurse   I can spit when I want to   thank
      you
no   not a particle of pain

what time is it?
my God   is that all?   let me see
I went into the operating-room at eight
and you say it's only eleven now?
isn't time funny!   yes   funny was what I said
you know   nurse
I'm really much nicer than you'd think   seeing me in this
      ridiculous pickle
and I want you to tell me honestly and frankly

the operation is finished   isn't it?
yes   I believe you   but it seems incredible
he's a swell guy   that man
you know   nurse   I think he's probably the greatest sur-
    geon in the world
I am always attracted by these really brilliant Jewish types
are you Jewish too?

oh my God   nurse!   there it comes!
that's the real pain   all right   all right
oh nurse! . . .

now   wasn't it cute of you to have the hypodermic all
    ready!
you certainly have a skillful quick touch
I didn't even feel the needle go in

(3)

hours and hours will drift along
clicks the dull electric fan
listen to my lovely song
make of it all things you can
fan and fan and fan is fannie
hear   the tune   O little mannie
hear the melodies that throng
down the night   it will be long

18

fan and man and buzz and turn
water drown and fire burn
   "in fernem Land   weit fort von euren Schritten" . . .
   "with rue my heart is laden   for golden friends I had"

   . . .

   "yet once more   O ye laurels   and once more   ye
      myrtles brown with ivy never sere" . . .
   "I am the rose of Sharon   and the lily of the valleys"

   . . .

fan and fan and fan is fan
there's no help   my little man

(4)

shrieking up and down the interminable hours of the night
come the echoes   the reverberations   the cries
from the room across the corridor I hear the groans and
      babblings
of a man emerging from the brief respite of ether
a child across the courtyard is screaming in terror   on the
      floor above me
lights suddenly flash dim haloes in the misty night air   and
I can hear the words   the silences   I can almost hear the
      rumble
of the smooth rubber-tired truck that bears away
that patient to the elevator   and then down into the sudden
      glare

of prismed reflectors in the operating-room   where four chattering nurses
amid the deadly stench of ether
rattle knives and scissors and forceps and basins
and a sullen anaesthetist waits boredly
until the great surgeon   summoned from his tired bed at midnight
enters   alert calm controlled silent   his two assistants follow
all of them white from head to foot   and masked like monsters
they touch nothing
the great surgeon says "go ahead with the anaesthetic doctor
Dr Morris   you will be at my left   Dr Jamieson opposite
I am ready   Miss Heath"

the hundreds of rooms in this hospital vibrate night and day
I hear   I feel it all
I hear   I feel the same pulsation
in a thousand other hospitals near and far
I feel the pain of a woman dying of cancer untended in India
and the numbness of a man freezing to death on the plains of Siberia
and the shudders of a man in Detroit who was sprayed with burning oil

this hospital is a howling chaos
whither all voices come

the hours pass on

Betelgeuse and Sirius and the Pleiades change their places
in the sky

and the sun is perhaps sending down a calm evening light
on China

as this minute speck of stone and water turns in its dizzy
course

I must think of something   I must think of something
quickly

for I shall go mad rather soon if I let my mind remain a
vacuum for pain

I will think of the tall bamboo forests and crystal brooks of
Mokanshan

where I used to pursue the huge black-and-gold butterflies

through the glow of tropic afternoons   and bathe naked in
the streams

or I will think of the days when through storm and
sun

I sailed among the Aegean Isles   and ate harsh bread and
cheese and olives

and drank the resin-flavored wine of the fishermen

and shared their danger and was their friend

or I will recall the days and nights when I lived in an attic
in Paris overlooking a secret garden

and knew love and beauty like a privileged god

no   I cannot think of these things for more than a moment
my mind will not answer my commands
come on then   devils!

(6)

thank God I am here alone   thank God that no one who
     loves me
is hovering about   doubling my pain by letting me see it
     reflected
in the mirror of her sensitive face

when I confront certain dark powers I would do so in soli-
     tude
then can I fight better
being unburdened by the fear that my weakness and ig-
     nominy be seen

(7)

oh   good evening   doctor   you are the intern for this
     floor?
sit down and have a cigarette   yes I'm all right   thank you

yes   I had noticed those lighted numbers that flash on and
     off
on the bulletin-board in the hall
no   I have not the slightest idea what they are for
oh   they are floor-signals for doctors and nurses   are they?
no   I do not think that number thirteen has come up yet

22

why do you smile when you say that it will come up soon?
oh   number thirteen means that an autopsy is going on in
      the basement, does it?
thirteen   the unlucky number   why of course!
you doctors have indeed a great sense of humor

it all sounds rather grim as you tell about it
this taking out of the heart   the brain
the lungs   the guts   the entire spine and so forth
your phrase is wonderfully descriptive of the picture
"a circle of carrion-crows around a dead sheep!"
but I think what impresses me most in your story
is the fact that you then fill up the empty skull with concrete
"as a courtesy to the undertaker and the relatives"
you doctors   for all your virtues   seem to me an odd lot
you're not quite human   you get a little warped
there's more of the mischievous ape left in you than you sus-
      pect
I think that about half of you are about half-crazy

no   doctor   I think I will decline your courteous invitation
to come to the basement with you some night when I am
      better
and watch an autopsy
do not misunderstand me   if I died tonight you boys
would be quite welcome to play your pranks with my useless
      tissues
but I would really prefer not to be present in person

23

the child in the room opposite mine
screamed all day and most of the night and all the next day

as I fought minute after minute and hour after hour against
    my own pain
I wanted to scream   too   and I wanted to kill that child

in the dusk of the second evening—
in that hour when hospital-corridors are ghostly with
the quiet footfalls of departing visitors and with
the voices of nurses coming on duty or going off duty   and
    there are audible
the faint sounds of motor-horns and radios from the outside
    world—
then in the child's room I heard music

it was a richly male   very beautiful voice   singing
an old German folk-lullaby   a Jewish male voice
as gentle as a woman's   and full of honey and tears   and it
    sang
    "gute Nacht   mein liebes Kind
    gute Nacht   mein liebes Kind" . . .
on and on through the endless tender stanzas
that breathed unbearable love like a benediction
as the song rehearsed the pictures of the sunny play-hours
    of the day

the flowers   the trees   the birds   the slow-closing after-
      noon
and the coming of tranquil night
      "gute Nacht   mein liebes Kind"
superbly the male voice chanted on
pouring out a passion that was no less rich than life-blood
and slowly·   as the end of the song drew nearer
the voice grew lower   softer   as perhaps the eyes of the
      child closed
      "gute Nacht   mein liebes Kind
      gute Nacht   mein liebes Kind" . . .
and then as the powerful voice hushed itself to a whisper
the control was lost
and the man croaked like a raven
and his singing ceased

two days later
the child's voice   too   was silent

                        (9)
"good evening   I am sorry to say that I have bad news for
      you
I wish I could let you off   but I cannot
there are indications of a possible infection
in such a case I have no choice
I shall operate again at eight o'clock tomorrow morning"

                         25

howling hell!   howling hell!

oh   very well   oh   very well

but if anybody thinks I can stand the pressure of this new
    dressing

they're just mistaken   that's all   that's all

yes   I will ring once more for a nurse

and if she doesn't come in five minutes

I'm going to get out of bed and walk down those four flights
    of stairs

and stand in the middle of the street and howl like a dog

I'm going to howl—   I want a doctor   I want a doctor

and I can't get one in this god-damn hospital

that will shame them   that will shame them

I said to myself

a nurse came   a dumb one

and I said—   a hypodermic   quick!

and she said—   "I don't know whether you can have
    one"

and I said—   "you'd better know   you'd better know!

go look at my chart and you'll find out"

and she came back and said—   "I can't find your chart   it
    isn't there"

and I said—   get an intern   get an intern

he can give an order for morphine   you'd better hurry

and she said— "Oke" and went away
and I never saw her again
probably she thought it wasn't very good policy
for a nurse to wake up an intern at three-thirty in the morn-
    ing
and patients rarely raise rows about such things
patients go away very soon but interns last forever

so I got no morphine that night
and I sincerely hope that this particular nurse
gets no water in hell

(11)

"now turn over on yer right side
so's I can wash yer back
that's right   dear

yes   I was in the war
I was just a girl then   in training in Dublin
they sent me right over to France
yes   it was pretty hard work   we had too many cases
and it wasn't a right hospital at all   just boards

no   I don't remember anything special about it
no   I didn't meet any romantic heroes
most of them were pretty sick
we had a few German officers   and they were nice

27

they seemed so surprised and grateful when you did things
    for them
our orders was to treat them just the same as anybody else
well   why not?   they're human
there was one of them who spoke wonderful English
he was always quoting Shakespeare at me
he was a card   he died

now turn over on yer back   dear
so's I can wash yer front

what?   oh everybody always asks you that question
about whether men or women patients are worse
of course when a woman asks you you've got to say that
    there's no difference
but it ain't true
take it from me   women are bitches
no pity   no mercy   when they get a nurse in their clutches
bitches   I'm telling you

have you been in a hospital before?   oh yes   well then
    you'll know
you take this wash-cloth and wash down-below
I'll be right back

did you wash all right?   that's fine   dear
no I didn't mean not to answer your question about

my having a good time with men
but the truth is   I don't like men very much that way
I'd rather have the smell of a good cigar anytime

well   good-night dear   hope you sleep   but if you don't
just push the button   there's an order on your chart
for a half-grain every four hours if you need it"

(12)

I wonder what the real relations are
between all the temporary ghosts
that pass up and down these bare corridors

is the quiet prim little floor-superintendent liked
or do all the twenty-five nurses on this floor
stalk the corridors with knives under their white blouses
waiting until she makes a mistake   and they can strike to
      kill?
is that very beautiful dark-eyed nurse with the Italian name
who is so conscious of her breasts
really trying to get up an affair with me or am I just flattering
      myself?
which of the nurses slept last night with which intern or
      doctor?
that tall placid blonde one slept with somebody   I am sure
for her satisfied smile as she washed me this morning
was musical and monumental

29

do these women admire the surgeons whom they serve so
    attentively
or do they note and remember their mistakes
and regard them as a lot of pretentious boobs?
where   when   and how do they have their love-affairs?—
in their own rooms in the nurses' wing of the hospital
or in hotel-rooms
or furtively in the linen-closet when the halls are silent?
how much money does that skinny tired-looking nurse
manage to save out of her salary and send to her adored
    nephew
to play at the races?
how does that whale-shaped nurse
manage to waddle about these halls so many hours a day
without crying out to all the world how her feet hurt
    her?
what are their hopes?   what are their fears?   what meaning
do they derive from life as they see it in this madhouse
of shrieking pain and noble devotion and unfair bureauc-
    racy and severe science?
what price do they pay for their unshrinking callousness?
are they human?   if you pricked them   would they bleed?

some   I think   would not
but there are others   I think   who would bleed to death
if you merely touched their pulses with understanding
    fingers

Thank you so much   Miss Cohn   Miss Murphy   Miss
    Jones   Miss Amendetara

thank you so much   Dr Bernstein   Dr Jamieson   Dr
    Morgan

yes   I am glad to go   of course   even though you have
    all been so kind

yes   I shall come back someday to visit you here in your
    world

that is not the real world—   a world perhaps more real
    or more horrible

or more beautiful—   I do not know—   than the real world

But I am glad to go now

you are serious?

you really mean that the rules of the hospital

oblige me to sit in that wheeled chair and be carted to the
    door of exit?

you mean that though I am big enough to knock you all flat

I am to ride like a baby in its perambulator to the door?

very well!   how wonderful!

life is wonderful   death is wonderful   everything is won-
    derful

MEXICAN LAKE

THIS lake, Chapala,
Is of Time, not of Space only:
It partakes of two existences.
Even when visible here before me
It is like a memory.

    Today—tomorrow—yesterday . . .
The lake has its quiet surfaces,
The hills have their solid protuberances,
The valleys have their secret depths
Wherein unknowable life is nourished.
Sun and shadow play facilely along these beaches;
And great islands of lyrios, the water-hyacinths,
Float in from the far margins;
And sometimes the sunsets are like volcanoes of flame.

    Sometimes there comes a grey day
When the farther shore
Is as remote as the shore of an ocean.
Sometimes there comes a sunny day

When the mountains approach, and intrude at your window,
And you could touch the farther shore with your out-
  stretched hand.

  Quiet dark-eyed fishermen sail over these waters
And dip their nets into the lake
Or drowse along the beach.
In the market-place, vendors of pottery
Peer up hopefully from the dusty ground
Where they sit beside their little piles of wares.
Along the roadways, burros laden with corn-husks or sugar-
  cane
Trudge reluctantly beside their somnolent owners.
A hush broods over this lake.
Many races of men have lived upon its shores,
And the lake is older than any race of man.
When the mountains grow weary of struggling with the
  moon
And the earthquakes ride howling over and under the earth,
Then this lake will slip sideways like a seagull
And bring peaceful sleep to many sad-eyed men.

(2)

  And you, my friend,
With the sensitive aquiline old profile of George Meredith—
You who sit all day
With your dirty bare feet in the gutter

And sell peanuts, twenty peanuts for a copper coin,
And go home at night to your reed hut
With perhaps fifteen coppers as your sole possession—
What do you think of this business of being alive?

(3)

The blind girl stands, motionless and beautiful,
Every evening at the foot of the stair
That leads up to the beer-pavilion where the gay blades of
Guadalajara
Come in motors with their floosies to dance.
She murmurs a quiet entreaty
As each person passes by.
Some give her a small coin,
Some do not.

(4)

In the glaring whiteness of the moonlit street tonight
I passed a happy man.
He was ragged, he was singing, as he bumped from wall to
wall
Of the narrow highway.
As we approached each other, he, a stranger,
Hailed me as "Amigo!"
And we affectionately embraced for a moment
Before he staggered on his way down the moonlit street
And was gone from my sight forever.

At sunset, when at one end of the lake
The great clouds ride in fire,
While yonder in mists the ambiguous Lords of Tlalocan
Brood darkly over man—
Then I, a wondering stranger, a heathen,
Begin to understand that there are gods,
And that man, being weak and wicked, desires them.

(6)

The bells of the tall white Spanish church
From their two filagreed towers
Clang loudly in raucous discords, like cow-bells.
Inside, before the candle-lighted altar,
The priest, with a face like a pig,
Performs holy rites
While hundreds of sad black-clad women kneel in awe.
In front of the church, four soldiers with rifles
And heavy ammunition-belts
Pace uncertainly to and fro
Wondering whether they should interfere
And whether the government meant what it said when it
said
That the churches had been closed forever.

The stars at night, on this lake,
Are clearer than the daylight—
Steady, silent,
Less mysterious,
Less ominous,
Closer to my heart: I can understand the silence.

I found a little head of baked clay
In the ploughed fields.
The face was smiling; above the face
Was a half-withdrawn mask depicting a skull—
The mask of Mictlan-tecutli, Lord of the Dead.
And then across ten centuries of time
I stared into the eyes of my brother, the man who had made
        this image—
And was astonished that I had a brother.

9

The two policemen, shouldering their rifles,
Were gay and kind this evening
As they sympathetically dragged the drunken peasant out
        of the gutter
And carried him to his hut—and while he snored
Said inviting amorous words to his stolid wife.

His wife frankly indicated
That she was seven months gone in pregnancy, and was
    sorry she couldn't.
So, with perfect good temper, the soldiers
Departed laughing.

(10)

The villages around this lake
Have names that echo with a far-off music.

Some of them have names that are harsh
With the barbaric splendor of Aztec words—
Mexcala, Tizapan, Tuxcueca,
Ocotlan, Jocotopec—
Names with the fierce brightness of obsidian swords.

Side by side with them are villages
That have the softer Spanish names—
San Pedro Caro, Santa Cruz, San Nicholas,
San Cristobal, Santa Cruz de la Solidad, San Antonio—
Names echoing the music of a homeland
Which many of the Spanish conquistadores
Were never to see again.

And there are also villages in whose names
Two voices seem to mingle—
San Juan Tecomatlan, San Pedro Tizistan, San Juan Co-
    zala—

Villages where you will see fair-haired blue-eyed girls
Playing in the streets with black-haired girls
Whose eyes are darkness.

(11)

O strange funereal image which I bought from a boy to-
    day—
Image out of some ancient tomb—
You, image, seated with folded arms—
You, looking down the end of your long nose
With puzzled melancholy eyes—
You, lost in meditation:
Who were you?   What life did you live?   What death did
    you die?
Answer me, image!   Tell me of the grave in which you lay
For a thousand years.
Tell me of the spirit you represent in the Land of the Dead,
Tell me of the hope, the hands, that made you in the Land
    of the Living.
Speak, image!   For I will listen to all your words
With attentive ears.
Speak, my friend!   For I also have a long nose
And puzzled eyes.

(12)

I saw the Easter festival in the plaza last night
Amid the lights of colored lanterns and torches.
It was gay and charming; but I was tired, and left early.

This morning three corpses were carried past my gate—
The result of drinks and shooting that started late at night.
I expressed to my servant Ysidoro the opinion
That it was impolite to murder people.
But Ysidoro shook his head and disagreed.
He said that there were many people in the world
Who ought to be killed.
When I asked him if he himself had ever killed anyone
He replied that he had not.
But after a moment of honest reflection, he added
That he had once cut off a man's ear.

(13)

　　With patched square-rigged sails
And prows high and sharp as a blackbird's beak
The long dark boats of the fishermen
Move slowly out into the sunlight of the wide lake.
They will return at evening,
The dark hulls blacker, the white sails more silver
Against the golden light of the west.
And they will hang their nets on poles along the beach
While the moon comes up in the east
And turns the nets to spider-webs of silver.

(14)

　　Sometimes winds sweep over this lake
And vast waves dash upon the shores

While a calm sunset shines in the west
And the grey mountains are streaked with gold.
Do not try to understand this lake.
No man has ever understood it.
Take it into your heart and be one with it,
And let it take you into its heart and be one with you.

(15)

Beautiful trees live beside this lake.— The pepper tree
With its delicate drooping leaves like maidenhair fern
And its clusters of small red berries—
The rubber tree with its broad glossy leaves
As thick as saucers—the banana tree
Waving its tattered elephant-ears in the wind—
The cocoanut palm thrusting high into the air
Its arrowlike shaft and plumed crest—the mango
With heavy clustering foliage of dark green—the jacaranda
Suddenly on a season adorning its bare bony twigs
With translucent clouds of lavender-colored flowers.

In the tangles of the jungles that lie far southward,
These trees battle together in a deadly struggle for life.
But here on the edges of this lake
They rise in separate and tranquil beauty
As if nature held in its heart no evil.

16

It seems at times as though this lake, these shores,
Were trying to say something to me.
What is it that they would utter?
Is it that the life of man
Is brief and dreamlike as a cloud-shadow on the water,
And that it is well that the heart of man
Should peacefully brood here in the quiet sunshine,
Perturbing itself not
With anguish of hopeless hopes
And vain regrets?
Strive not to speak, O lake, O shores;
That which you would say was already known to me.

17

As the peasant came to me today
Bringing for sale the obsidian sacrificial knife
Which he had found in the fields,
I looked into his face and was terrified;
For the dark sharp profile,
The burning eyes and the cruel lips,
Were none other than the lineaments of the Aztec priest
Who had once wielded this knife
And lifted up the hearts of victims toward the sun.

In the twilight, bats dart in swift flight
Under the boughs of the great trees of my garden.

They seem like spirits of the darkness.
But my servant Ysidoro tells me that this is not so.
He says it is a well-known fact
That they are rats who have grown old.

(19)

One should not give money to beggars.
Today an irresistible impulse
Made me give a peso to a very old woman
Who, folded in her tattered shawl,
Looked so frail that the light almost shone through her.
As I turned quickly and shamefacedly away,
Her astonished outpouring of gratitude and prayers for my
    soul
Followed me with haunting anguish—
And then changed in the air, and I fancied that I heard far-
    off
Howls and maledictions,
The voice of all the misery of the world.

(20)

A reed hut ten feet square,
A pig, six chickens, a burro,
A bean-patch and a corn-patch,
A wife, five children, and one more child in every coming
    year,

The bells of the church, the weekly music in the plaza—
What more, save for the wickedness of the tax-collector,
Could man desire?

(21)

Ysidoro, you are young and I am old
And the many hours of the day lie between us.
Yet tonight, in the sunset, as you bring me my drink,
You laugh at me
And I laugh at you;
And I am not entirely sure that we are not of the same age.

(22)

Lords of this lake!   Lords brooding over the lake
Most visibly in the evening!   Give us our daily bread;
Give us the power to take our brother's hand in kindness;
Grant us the strength to forgive ourselves our sins;
Fortify our courage—that we may love life
And fear not pain and old-age and death,
And that we may walk quietly in our own paths without
    evil.   Amen.

IV: BERKSHIRE SOLITUDES

THE GRANITE MOUNTAIN

SOIL, and small pebbles, and loose stones
Are proper to the fields below.
But here the earth's harsh granite bones
Jut naked into sun and snow.

The wind sweeps round them.   Night and day
With alternate and soundless beat
Go past, while skies turn blue or grey—
Crystal with cold or dim with heat.

Incorrigibly strong they stand.
A little of them washes down
To fertilize the farmer's land
Or choke the drain-pipes of the town;

But as the swift procession moves
With feet or fins or fangs or wings,
Like men or beasts, like hates or loves,
The rocks last longer than most things.

Around them farmers till the fields
Where other farmers on a time
Were busy; orchards grow, where yields
Of other orchards in their prime

Were proud across the countryside;
New trout gasp in the newborn stream.
Only these bitter rocks abide,
Rapt in their own peculiar dream.

THE HILLS

FOR MEN grown sick of noise and stress
The ancient hilltops wait,
As calm and as ambiguous
As mortal fate.

Here in the spacious airs of spring
Men walk the heights, and find
As in a mirror what they bring—
If not too blind.

MARCH NIGHT

SWIFT howling darkness sweeps the land.
High up upon the hills
Cry out the powers of cold and wind
Whose bitter passion kills.

It kills the stalk within the soil,
The bud within the sheath,
The blossom faint upon the bough,
The welling sap beneath.

In such a night of bitter wind
Tearing the hills apart,
Nothing can save the man who walks
With winter in his heart.

MIST

THE MIST came from an unknown place
And took the world away.
I woke at dawn to see my hills,
But all I saw was grey—

As limitless as time or space,
Vague as a maniac's dream.
The mist had borne my world away
On its insensate stream.

I turned my head and slept again—
Sleep is a sovereign art—
And when I woke, the hostile mist
Was blown, was strewn apart—

And I walked forth and saw my hills,
Trod them, and was content.
Yet still I dreamed a dream of mists
And what their coming meant.

I dreamed that in no lesser mist
The heart forever moves,
Seeing as vague ambiguous shapes
The forms it hates or loves—

And sees not clearly ever once
In this fog-haunted place
The actual sun, the actual hills,
Or the friend's actual face.

WHEN in the woods the small white trillium-flower
After long seasons of the snow and rain
Gleams in the dead moss, and a sudden hour
Of light is in the storm-clouds, and again
Birds make their nests under the southern eaves,
And sun and hail are alternate in the sky,
And the apple-tree with blossoms hides its leaves,
And night is tremulous with the marsh-frog's cry—
Then by these signs men know another Spring
Has come upon the land, and are content.
Winter is now a gone forgotten thing
As earth awakens to new merriment.
Earth has no memory: the glad birds sing
The song of last year's birds, who came and went.

LANDSCAPE

BEAUTIFUL HILLS, beautiful hills around me!
Always remote though daily I walk your summits,
Always silent as if with the hush preceding
The moment of speech—

  Always like friends about me, as if to tell me
That you will speak the speech that is native to you
When, on a day, I shall be part of your substance,
Silent like you.

APRIL WINDS

ON THIS my stony slope of mountain
The wind was wild today,
Shaking dead grasses and grim bony trees,
Like the excited play

Of maenads come among the older gods
Whose sage and hoary hair
They toss and tumble with the liberty
Allowed the young and fair.

Old gods, old granite gods! it is in vain
You frown: the revered head
Wins no respect from these gay willful power
That laugh at all things dead.

MAY

WHEN apple-trees like naked girls
Laugh gay beneath the sun,
And the more sober chestnut lifts
Its candles one by one,

And the grey hillsides turn to brown
Behind the deep-sunk plow,
And green begins to haunt the birch
White on the hilltop's brow,

And every lilac is in flower—
Then steel your heart for pain
As the inexorable power
Of life blooms back again.

THE RABBIT

HE CAME, a thief in the night
With footfall light.

And in the early dawn
I saw my garden gone.

And that same afternoon,
And not an hour too soon,

I caught him in the snap
Of a fierce trap,

And found him waiting thus,
Held tremulous,

A manifest culprit, there
Caught by the hair.

And then I suffered so,
I let him go.

THE SNAKE

WITH PATTERNED MOTTLINGS of diagonal scales,
    his head
Rose up slowly out of the water-cress.
Sickened, I struck—and he lay writhing, dead.
And I knew less
Of why I struck than he, dying slowly, knew
Of why he had been smitten, by what thunder.

  In a bewildered silence I still view
My deed with wonder. . . .

MIDSUMMER

THIS EXCELLENCE of summer weather,
When on the hills the friendly sun
Calls out—"Throw off your clothes and run,
A savage gone mad altogether!—

   "And cry beneath the blazing noon
A chant of deeper-voiced content
Than any fool who ever went
Raving beneath the pallid moon."—

   When in the air the golden heat
With coolness of the wind conspires
To fill the sky with dumb desires
And make earth natural to the feet—

   With my remaining wisdom then
I covet, spite of all their ills,
What stupid cattle on the hills
Know beyond consciousness of men.

CAROLINE, A HORSE

WHAT LIVES behind those eloquent eyes
Is neither prescient—souled nor wise—
A glow that faintly lives or dies.

So beautiful! And yet no thought
Into those fibers was inwrought.
As iron is bent, so was she taught

By alternating praise and blow
The few small things her brain can know,
Beyond whose bound she cannot go.

And I, whose strength is nothing, rule
This mighty, breathing, plunging fool
And put her terrible force to school—

I whose vague flickering brain can see
So little of that mystery
Of mighty powers that govern me.

Yet take, O heart, thy moment's pride:
The horse and I, with me to guide—
See how triumphantly we ride!

THE TOILER

HE WORKS from dawn to dusk in the small field,
Destroying the hostile weed,
Planting once more the hopeful seed,
Patiently looking toward the eventual yield.

He notes the oncoming of the wished-for rain
Or of the hated frost.
He toils transfixed and lost;
The summer's beauty blooms for him in vain.

Never in all his laboring anxious years
Has he looked toward the sky
Save as an omen that will prophesy
The dubious measure of his hopes and fears.

The glowing instant, the immortal hue
Special to dawn or dusk or night or noon—
The depth of shadows underneath the moon,
The sunset green—are things he never knew.

And past him flows the unreturning stream
Of time, transparent as the evening air;
And death will come before he grows aware
Of the sharp colors of the mortal dream.

EXILED FROM EDEN

THE SMILING MASK that Nature wears
Is hers but to betray.
Fiends hide behind this Eden's leaves.
Angels have fled away.

To Eden's gate, man, long exiled,
Returns not as of old.
He marvels at that trusting child
Of the Age of Gold.

In calm refusal he denies
Kinship with purposes
That shake the earth with anguished cries
And drown in blood the seas.

On days of light he wanders forth,
But is no more at one
With meadows stretching south and north
Under the sun.

He shudders when small hares cry shrilly
In grip of the hawk's claws.
He turns from where the water-lily
Hides the pike's jaws.

He contemplates with no consenting
The million-terrored earth,
Hearing the chorus of lamenting
Of lives foredoomed from birth:—

The deer by the rock-viper slain;
The snake in agony
Dragging its endless day of pain
To where night lets it die;

The fox, that fed on living things,
Now trapped flesh, dying;
The wild bird lost on crippled wing,
Desperately crying;

The mayfly from the water born
To dart once in the sun
Until before the morrow's morn
Its course is run;

The carp that feasts upon her young;
The worm that best will thrive
In the carp's gills, and there among
Deaths, grow alive;

The unimagined multitude
Of forms in every pool and stream,
Avid for life, avid for blood,
As in an evil dream.

Man walks the hills with heavy heart,
Finding in all he sees
No mirror and no counterpart
Of his sole fantasies.

The pity that his brain devised
Is his alone:
The bread his foolish heart surmised,
Is gritty stone.

THE CURSE OF ADAM

LET not the mortal heart in grief
Pity the transient butterfly.
Although its hour of life is brief
It does not know that it can die.
Never in shadows of a dream
Do there come whispering ominously
To aught that stirs in wood or stream
Rumors that it shall cease to be.
Of all the forms that live and move
Under the terms of blood and breath,
Man, only, through the summer grove
Hears the far wind of certain death.

HE now accepts the solitude
As he accepted Spring.
This region of a graver mood
Is no more strange a thing
Than April was in arrogant green
Or Summer's golden prime.
His eyes have seen what they have seen,
Each in its destined time.
Now Winter threatening on the hills,
Darkening the roads below,
Brings him no unawaited ills.
He knows what he must know.

THE DEAD TREE

BLEAK, bony-grey, its twisted branches rise
To stab in lightning-patterns at the skies.
Whatever else may die, it no more dies.

   Triumphant and defiant there it stands;
Of Spring it makes no further brief demands;
It towers a monument above the lands.

   It will return to that earth whence it came;
But now, a few years, like a frozen flame,
It spreads gigantic branches to proclaim

   The swift dispersal of all life's distress
Whether the seasons smite or if they bless:—
The innocence of ultimate Nothingness.

FALLEN ROBIN'S-NEST

GRIEVE not for Nature: that abyss of pain
Is an imputed one.
The wind-swept robin's-nest was not in vain
Built in the triumph of the air and sun.
Wrecked now and low it lies,
Ruined for our dim eyes;
But for an hour it was her destined throne.

   And for that hour, life rose to ecstasy,
Burned bright, and sang in her tumultuous breast.
Powers prisoned in the dust were there set free
Into an unimagined mystery.
What matter though the nest
From its high branch brought low
Now in pale ruin lies?
Once there was triumph and not overthrow—
A burst of joy beneath the indifferent skies.

SUNLIGHT ON A BROOK

FLICKER of sunlight on the rapid brook
In this secluded rock-bound nook—

And in a sudden miracle of fusion
Light, water, I, meet in the brief illusion

Of beauty, for my transitory sense—
Then hurry on. . . .

A million light-years hence
Perhaps we three shall meet, after vast range.
And I, for one, shall find the meeting strange.

O BEAUTY INFINITE

O BEAUTY infinite, that in all things
Implicit and discoverable lies—
That glimmers, flows, emerges, hovers, sings—
Sleeps in the rock, and in the bird-note cries—
Sometimes obscured in the thick night of pain,
Forgotten sometimes by the desperate mood
Of him who wanders in too dark a wood—
But on some day illuminate again!

I think that when my eyes were very young
I saw You clearly for a little while
In evening-firelight and my mother's smile:
I saw how did unclose
In every Spring each petal of the rose
And heard each dawn-swept bird-note that was sung.
But grown to man's estate
These things were mine no more; and unaware
Of these small wonders I beheld my fate,
That possible fabric of my love and hate,
As the sole miracle hovering in the air.

Now in the pauses of a later day,
When without taint of hope or bitterness
I acquiesce
To the foredoomed distress
That waits for each man in his separate way—
Now I recover wonders so well known
When I was but an ignorant dreaming child.
And though tomorrow come wind-swept and wild,
I shall find something there that is my own.

I shall revert sometime, and be at ease
With spectral shadows of the clouds and trees
And intimate with secrets of the rain.
Today, amid the waste of useless hours
I almost saw in simple roadside flowers
A beauty not of wisdom nor of pain.

V: CELESTIAL PRESENCES

TO JOHN COWPER POWYS

AGAIN upon this hill we meet
As in so many an earlier time.
Not friendship, now, has grown less sweet
Nor the fantastic lure of rhyme
Nor clouds nor birds nor anything
Within our earliest youthful ken.
So let us be alone, and fling
Away the wickedness of men;
And in the gentleness of a mood
Not lost to us, though all forget,
Pledge with a sober quietude
The distant days when first we met—
Our equal lust for passing hours
That are so lovely as they pass—
Our equal faith in certain powers
Seen, ah how darkly! through a glass.

FROM THE OLD CITY you have emerged; the high
    towers
Are only a memory now; the vast prison-like rooms
Are only a memory; the terrifying word of the captains
No longer is the wise word.

    Now relinquish everything; relinquish the heart's pride,
        and the secrecy
Of old confusions; let fall the old humiliations,
The doubts, the fears, the arrogances, the disgraces;
Hold nothing back.

    For this is a sunlight into which you have come, proudly
        and humbly;
And you enter it flower-crowned and naked;
And there are songs in the branches, and flowers where your
        foot falls,
And darkness is dead.

    Here in this meadow where you walk defenceless,
Here where the fields lie open, and not a wall
Or an armed watch on the rampart is strong to guard you—
Here, my belovèd, you are safe.

TO A LADY WHO LOVES GARDENS

DO NOT tend the flowers in your garden tonight: come
 talk with me instead.
Do not toil to oppose the whim of Nature
Or to put one plant in place of another plant in your garden.
If need be, let the weeds grow up,
Let the dandelions overpower the violets;
Are not the delicate anemones yonder in the woods enough?
Tonight let your compassion desert your garden for a little
 while.
Come walk with me, instead, on the hilltop.
Overhead there is always the sky, and the granite is under-
 foot,
And much is to be spoken. Postpone the garden. Let
 there be no garden.
So long as you walk the earth, the earth is my garden,
And that garden will be beautiful to me so long as you walk
 in it.

SPEAK OUT YOUR LOVE

BEFORE the sure-departing ships
Are scattered to the farthest lands,
Speak with your heart and with your lips
And with the pressure of your hands.

Speak out your love! Let it not hide
Like a lost ship in deeps profound
Among the bones of things that died,
Untouched by light, bereft of sound.

Here in the perilous lands of hate
Postpone the doubts that make you wise,
And look before it is too late
With utter love into loved eyes;

Lest on some unexpected day
When a ship sails, to come no more,
The watcher by the empty bay
Pace silent up and down the shore.

PRAYER FOR A LADY

HERE in the high midsummer hour
I call upon Thy Grace and Power.

O Lord, Thy benefice confer
On me, but most of all on her

Whose delicate untroubled face
Is as the mirror of Thy Grace,

A gift not to be known or spoken,
A light, a metaphor, a token

Of love we shall not wholly say
Through the long eloquence of the day.

This prayer I offer unto Thee
Aware of its futility.

Full well I know Thou canst do naught,
Being but a figment of my thought.

It is a folly, that I seek
Thy Voice, where there is none to speak.

And yet, dear Lord, so much her worth
In the confusions of the earth

That prayers for her sake must be said
Even though God himself is dead.

Wherefore, dear Lord, Thy Blessing give
On her, Thy angel-fugitive.

NURSERY RHYME

LADY-BUG, lady-bug, will you be mine?
I'll feed you on apples and buttercup-wine.
You shall sit on a cushion and sew a fine seam,
And I'll sing to you songs that I made in a dream.

I'll sing you of peacocks, and amethyst seas,
And clouds in the sky-world, and monkeys in trees,
And when I've sung all things on earth and above,
I'll sing you a song very softly of love.

And you will grow drowsy and creep to our nest.
And there I will sing you the song that is best,
Of silence and sighing and dusk and moonshine.
Lady-bug, lady-bug, will you be mine?

THE POOL

SHE STOOD as slim, as clear, as cool
As any birch beside this pool—
Then with a sudden curving dive
Made the dark water spring alive,
A million ripples, and the white
Flash of her body's free delight
As out across the reed-fringed bay
She plunged in swift and naked play.

I would rather be the eyes that look
On her in this secluded nook
Than see all fabled queens afar—
The one who made the Grecian war,
The one who wrought the doom of kings,
The one who broke the minstrel's strings,
The one belovèd of the Swan,
Or any of all the beauties gone.

Dripping with drops that chase and glide,
Once more above the water-side
She poises with a little smile,
Natural, as if free from guile.

But well, supremely well, she knows
That she is colored like a rose,
And that my eyes are not yet dull,
And that a rose is beautiful.

PICNIC

NEAR FLORENCE once upon a hill
When all the world was rent by ill
There were, so says Boccaccio's pen,
Some ladies and some gentlemen
Who, tired of cities packed with evil,
Consigned the loud world to the devil,
And far from all that discontent
Partook of private merriment.

To me, it seems they did no wrong
To lighten with an hour of song
And wanton mirth and revelry
One spot of earth's vast misery.
Had they been heroes, and gone down
To fight the plague-fire in the town,
Their deaths had been of no avail
Save rob us of a pleasant tale.
Nor do I think that we do ill
Who picnic now upon this hill.

THE OLD NATURE-LOVER

SLOWLY he toiled up the long hill, and turned
Sometimes for views back into the chill valley
Where the defeated trees of Autumn burned
Their splendid torches—signals for some rally
Of ghostly gods to his support. At last
He reached the crest and entered at my door.
There by the warm fire, holding my hand fast
In his lean hand, he said: "I much deplore
What you have often told me—that those things
Most tender, natural, grave and terrible—
The little weeds, the newts, the clouds, the wings,
The leaves—bring to your heart no parable!"
He looked at me with eyes troubled and dim.
And almost I loved nature, loving him.

THE TALES are all thrice-pondered tales
That can be told.
The agile mind no whit avails;
Earth's life is old.

Nor does the labored search of youth
For intricate words
Enrich the simple quiet truth
Of the few chords.

Vain are the novelties of surprise
That we invent.
In labyrinths of old surmise
Best be content,

Touching with dreaming hand the strings
Which long ago
Echoed those few, unchanging things
The heart can know.

TO MY MOTHER ON HER SEVENTY–THIRD BIRTHDAY

YOU ASK: "When does old age begin?"
When the heart's sympathy wears thin,
And in the contours of a face
Malice and hatred take their place;
When the perceptions of the mind
To hopes of younger hearts grow blind;
When the grim passion to possess
Becomes the source of happiness;
When the once-generous warmth is cold—
Then, then indeed, the heart is old.
But fear not! for I tell you true
This fate will never come to you.
The love that in your heart has sung
Will still sing on, and keep you young.

"DEARLY BELOVÈD BRETHREN, I beg of you,"
(As Cromwell once said,)
"To believe it possible that you may be mistaken."
And through this twilight, this darkening night
Of ignorance and cruelty,
Reject not the hope of a Light.
Let us secretly preserve the Holy Embers
Until the hour comes when those who were always our
        enemies
And who never believed in kindness or beauty
Shall have exhausted each other in futile battles.
They can defeat each other:
But we cannot ever be defeated.

   We are slippery, like fish or a drop of water
Or a bit of manure or an angel.
We are humble, we are proud, we are evasive and
        dangerous.
And when the wicked men of the earth have at last settled
        their battles
We shall be there on the wrecked battle-field
Offering them cups of water which we have treasured for
        them.

94

WHEN I remember my immortal dead
And see the eyes that in a former time
Looked at me, and recall the splendor shed
God-like by those tall figures in their prime—
And do not quite forget how one man spoke,
And how one strode, and how another stood
When the word came beneath which at a stroke
His lofty tree splintered to useless wood—
And how another, prouder than the rest,
Accepted once my hand in evil hour,
And how another from his own racked breast
Brought me a secret and most healing power—
Then I desire to live, at any cost,
Lest when I die these memories should be lost.

VI: VARIOUS PHANTOMS

AH, IT WAS YOU knocking upon the door!
Come in, old friend; sit down; rattle the chair
With your long bony knees; do not deplore
Your coming unannounced. I was aware
That you were wandering somewhere in these lands.
I greet you here tonight with no surprise.
You good old hardy visage! Your lean hands
Are firm as ever, deep as ever your eyes.
Rest here before my hearthfire for a while.
Much you could tell me that I do not know;
There are fantastic secrets in your smile:
You have learned gossip, wandering to and fro!
Sit down in the rich evening, and beguile
My fancy with your tales—before we go.

SOUL IN TORMENT

(John Donne, 1573–1631)

WHEN this my mortal course is run
And I withdraw to far retreat
Among the angels, there is one
I hope with all my heart to meet—
That worthy prelate Dr Donne
Strolling down the Celestial Street.

Incredible angel! so perplexed
By mysteries of good and evil
That God was surely sometimes vexed
And almost tossed thee to the Devil—
Who would immediate have unsexed
Thee, poet, in thy heights of revel.

Incredible mortal! in whose mind
Such richness of rebellion lay
That thy insatiate will must find
Some wickedest Babylonian way
For lust gone bitter, drunk and blind—
That thou mightst grieve the worse next day.

What wonder that thy earthly pain
Almost destroyed thy reason's sight?—
Thou snake that very near was slain
By venom of its own self-bite—
As thou didst lash to bloody stain
The quivering flanks of thy delight.

No armor ever could withstand
The awful arrows of thy wit;
All towers became but towers of sand
Where thy fierce cannon chose to hit;
Thou didst assail a godless land
Who wast the very nub of it:—

The keenest mind, the richest soul
That ever, weeping, did aspire
To heaven as its immortal goal
Out of the sweat of flesh-desire,
And saw the sacred planets roll
Licked round by meteors of hell-fire—

Crying, with anguish that would melt
The heart of God though it were stone,
That justice be not on thee dealt—
That Christ His Passion might atone!—
While for preferment thou didst pelt
With verse the whores round England's throne.

O thorny, glowing, twisted heart
That walked the London streets awhile
Singing thy song with subtle art
Of lust, repentance, fear and guile!
Thy guardian angel stood apart
And watched thee with a mocking smile—

Knowing that when thy sin was most
Then most didst thou exalt thy state,
Mad champion of that Holiest Ghost
That was in thee articulate.
Thy soul could never have been lost:
It stood all-time within The Gate.

ON DYING

I DOUBT if many when they die
Go from us as reluctantly
As is reputed. Men who dwell
Still in the sun odd stories tell
For mutual cheer, and sometimes strain
Truth to assuage their present pain
With legends of how dire it is
To enter to the mysteries
The farther side of death.

                      But they
Who from our lands have gone their way—
All whom I knew went cheerfully,
Not much unwilling to be free
From life's confused and manifold terror,
From the dim brain, the lurking error
Of cruelty in the kindest heart—
And lose the bitter separate part
Of Nature which in you and me
Creates our sole identity.

The rusted and dishonored sword,
The violated pledge, the word
Of foolish anger rashly spoken,
The once-heroic spear now broken,
The hatred which the spirit lays
On its defeated yesterdays—
These mark the tragedy of a line
Not, as it boasted, quite divine.

And weariness invades that breast
Whose friends, the noblest and the best,
Steal one by one voiceless away.
He can recall a happier day
Than this of growing solitude.
Some room or street or field or wood
Reminds his heart at savage cost
Of splendors dead, of beauties lost.

And everywhere, and everywhere,
In room or street, of earth or air,
Hunger and fear and agony
Stalk in the leering pageantry,
The carnival, the studied plan
Of man's vast cruelty to man.

We lie a little who pretend
Too much reluctance at the end.
All of the dead men that I know
Were glad with half their hearts to go.

A TOAST TO THE BUSHA GREY

WHEN Busha Grey walked down the road
His eyes turned back to me
As if he bore no heavy load
Of age and misery.
He waved a frivolous bony hand,
He smiled, he laughed at me.

He was a long cadaverous man;
His teeth were a disgrace;
A yellow look of death was on
His wanly jaundiced face;
Yet in his eyes a gleam of fun
Found an unseemly place.

I never saw such bright puttees
As Busha Grey then wore.
I never saw such well-washed shirts
As those which he upbore.
I never saw so calm a face
On the Jamaican shore.

Where people scurried to and fro
And busily came and went,
The Busha Grey paced lame and slow
On his own business bent
And seemed too old and wise to know
The lust of argument.

I know not if he walked with God
Or if he walked alone.
His eyes were eager, kind and just:
His lips were cold as stone.
Perhaps he had too many friends:
Perhaps he had not one.

When two awed Negroes lifted him
To sit his bony steed
He was the master, as of old;
He could command, and lead,
And die in some mad cavalry-charge
If that were then the need.

The Busha Grey knew very well
When last he took my hand
That we would never meet again
In any earthly land.
That thing he understood; not I:
I dared not understand.

And it was I, not he, who turned
And looked perplexed away—
I who was frightened by a hand
As lean and dry as clay—
I who dared not envisage then
The soon-approaching day.

Now Busha Grey is gone where none
Will drink with him again.
His gaiety now walks alone
In sunlight or in rain.
His wicked smile is calm: he'll not
Drink toasts with me again.

The high Jamaican hills among,
No wench was safe in days
When Busha Grey, delightful, young,
Went on his lusty ways
And fostered England's glory there
And God His proper Praise.

He drank his burning raucous rum
With any of the best.
He served the land whence he had come.
He slept upon the breast
Of every Negro wench who feared
The lash of his behest.

I knew him when his days were old
And his stiff legs were faint.
His hands were pitiful and cold.
Yet not like some pale saint
Did he repent, nor did he then
Utter one dull complaint.

He died upstanding as a man:
Repinings lay afar.
He said: "The race in which I ran
Was not to chase a star.
And so I end as I began.
And there, my friend, you are!"

Busha! I whisper you a word,
O most endearing ghost—
Not by a single ear now heard,
A word on the wind lost—
And raise my heavy glass of rum
And drink to you a toast!

To you, now sitting gay in Hell,
Your wrinkled eyes ashine,
While Satan's self is pleased full well
To welcome you to dine,
And many a ribald tale you tell
And quaff the fiery wine—

Recounting oddities of sin
You noted through the past
In various lands you wandered in—
Enlivening the vast
Hollow of Hell with friendly din
That hails you home at last.

TO A FRIEND WHO CHERISHES A VIAL OF POISON

(Accompanied by the gift of an ancient Japanese brocade)

THAT KEEN BLADE which the Samurai of old
Kept bright, to be his dear and ruthless friend
On some far day of sunlight growing cold
And honor's self coming to bitter end—
That blade he cherished in a silken sheath
Of curious workmanship, in quaint disguise
Of calm and ancient fabric; there beneath
The silk he guarded from the common eyes
His terrible, beloved, ancestral sword
Wherewith in last extremity could be stayed
Immitigable evils, and the word
Of time's worst insult quietly gainsaid . . .
Here, by safe messenger, I send, my lord,
A silken scabbard for your chosen blade.

THE HOUR–GLASS

THE ANCIENT MYSTERY of the falling sand
Pours down before me in the candle-light.
I hold the small toy in my powerful hand
As if it were a plaything—as if might
Of human will could wreck it with one sweep.
And yet, the wreckage done, quite well I know
A ghostly sand in slow increasing heap
Would trickle on into the space below.
The mortal earth is falling, grain by grain,
Each grain so little but the whole so dear.
No hand will turn the flow; never again
Reverse the hours of the brief human year;
Never again these golden sands will pass
From the one glass into the other glass.

WHEN I am old, and on my brain is laid
The rigor that precedes the one of death
And to my sight the slow-approaching shade
Has brought a dimness, and my difficult breath
No longer takes me to the highest hill
And I no more can wander in the wood
And naked by the brook suddenly thrill
With life of air and water; when my blood
Has ebbed to silence and I cannot hear
The winds go singing—then may winds that sung
Once in my heart be in my memory dear;
And may I never, looking on the young,
Say to them: "Wisdom is a tale untold
To hearts of young men, known but to the old."

FATHER

OH FATHER—if Thou wouldst indeed
Welcome Thy straying children home,
How eager were my heart to heed,
How humbly, gravely, would it come!

  I am no rude rebellious son
Contemptuous of Thy love's behest.
My broken fears would haste, would run
If Thou didst call me to Thy breast.

  Ah, in the midnight, in the dawn
I listened—and have never heard,
However faint or far-withdrawn,
The vibrance of Thy summoning word!

  More harsh than jangled bolts and bars—
More cruel than promises forgone—
The senile silence of Thy stars,
The idiot radiance of Thy dawn.

ABSOLUTION

CEASE, O my soul, with so perplexed a mood
To bear the burdens of the fate of man.
It was not you who made life's bad or good
Nor were your counsels asked when the firm plan
Was first established for the universe.
No guilt of yours with time and space conspired
To crush the better or exalt the worse:
That evil is, is not since you desired.
Take not upon yourself the heavy load
Of imperfection in the earth and sky
But humbly dwell within your small abode
And with unshrinking speculative eye
Watch through the doorway where along the road
The vast processions of the gods go by.

"THEN do you think," the gentle pastor said
As quietly we talked before the fire,
"That stone can serve the spirit as its bread
And lonely courage feed the heart's desire?
The natural life of man looks past the grave
For light that will illumine his dim terrors.
His faith cries out for Mercy that shall save
His blinded soul from its own doom of errors.
Let him believe for him his Savior died:
Else is his heart into the darkness thrust.
Even were it shown that all the Prophets lied,
Could man strive on without sustaining trust?"
The listener, in regretful voice, replied:
"I am not sure he can: I know he must."

THE END